Story

I can read the Speed sounds.

I can read the Green words.

I can read the Red words.

I can read the story.

I can answer the questions about the story.

I can read the Speed words.

Say the Speed sounds

Consonants

*Ask your child to say the sounds (not the letter names)
clearly and quickly, in and out of order. Make sure
he or she does not add 'uh' to the end of the sounds,
e.g. ' f' not 'fuh'.*

f	l	m	n	r	s	v	z	sh	th	ng nk

b	c k ck	d	g	h	j	p	qu	t	w	x	y	ch

Each box contains one sound.

Vowels

*Ask your child to say each vowel sound and then the word,
e.g. 'a' 'at'.*

at	hen	in	on	up

Story ⟨1⟩ Nog in the fog

Read the Green words

For each word ask your child to read the separate sounds, e.g. 'l-o-g' and then blend the sounds together to make the word, e.g. 'log'. Sometimes one sound is represented by more than one letter, e.g. 'th', 'sh', 'ck'. These are underlined.

can	run	and	in	fog
on	a	log	drip	drop

Ask your child to read the root word first and then the word with the ending.

trip → trips   jog → jogs

Read the Red words

Red words don't sound like they look. Read the word out to your child. Explain that he or she will have to stop and think about how to say the red word in the story.

<u>th</u>e

Story 1

Nog in the fog

Introduction

This rhyming story is about an alien called Nog who goes jogging.

Nog can run and
Nog can jog.

Nog jogs in the fog
and trips on a log.

Drip, drip, drop!

Ask your child:
What two things can Nog do?

Story 2 Grrrr!

Read the Green words

For each word ask your child to read the separate sounds, e.g. 'h-o-p' and then blend the sounds together to make the word, e.g. 'hop'. Sometimes one sound is represented by more than one letter, e.g. 'th', 'sh', 'ck'. These are underlined.

I   can   hop   fun   on   fat

tum   went   run

Ask your child to read the root word first and then the word with the ending.

it → it's

Read the Red words

Red words don't sound like they look. Read the words out to your child. Explain that he or she will have to stop and think about how to say the red words in the story.

s<u>ai</u>d   to

Grrrr!

Introduction

Do you like hopping? This rhyming story is about a mouse called Mop who likes to hop.

"I can hop," said Mop.
"I can hop, it's fun."

"It's fun to hop on Ted's fat tum."

"Grrrr!" went Ted.
Run, Mop, run!

Ask your child:
Why does Mop have to run?

Story ⟨3⟩ Sam gets a shock

Read the Green words

For each word ask your child to read the separate sounds, e.g. 'n-e-t', 's-o-ck' and then blend the sounds together to make the word, e.g. 'net', 'sock'. Sometimes one sound is represented by more than one letter, e.g. 'th', 'sh', 'ck'. These are underlined.

in   his   net   and   a   so<u>ck</u>

ro<u>ck</u>   <u>sh</u>o<u>ck</u>   nip

Ask your child to read the root word first and then the word with the ending.

dip → dips   get → gets

Read the Red words

Red words don't sound like they look. Read the word out to your child. Explain that he or she will have to stop and think about how to say the red word in the story.

he

Sam gets a shock

Introduction

Have you ever been fishing with a net? This rhyming story
is about a boy who gets a shock when he goes fishing.

Sam dips in his net and
gets a sock.

He dips in his net and gets a rock.

He dips in his net and gets a shock!

Nip, nip, nip!

Ask your child:
Why does Sam get a shock?

Story ⭐4 Push the bus

Read the Green words

*For each word ask your child to read the separate sounds, e.g. 'b-u-s',
'p-u-sh' and then blend the sounds together to make the word, e.g. 'bus',
'push'. Sometimes one sound is represented by more than one letter,
e.g. 'th', 'sh', 'ck'. These are underlined.*

pu<u>sh</u>   bus   is   stu<u>ck</u>   in   mud

and   mu<u>ck</u>   yuk

Read the Red words

*Red words don't sound like they look. Read the word out to your child.
Explain that he or she will have to stop and think about how to say the
red word in the story.*

<u>th</u>e

Story 4

Push the bus

Introduction
Have you ever got your feet stuck in mud?
This rhyming story is about a bus that gets stuck.

Push the bus. Push the bus. Push, push, push!

The bus is stuck
in mud and muck.

Push! Push! . . .

Yuk!

Ask your child:
 Where is the bus stuck?

Speed words for Story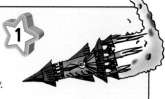

Ask your child to read the words across the rows, down the columns and in and out of order, clearly and quickly.

run	fog	trips	drip	can
and	jogs	log	drop	the

Speed words for Story

can	tum	went	on	fun
said	run	fat	hop	I

Speed words for Story 3

Ask your child to read the words across the rows, down the columns and in and out of order, clearly and quickly.

net	sock	in	and	dips
rock	his	nip	shock	gets

Speed words for Story 4

is	mud	bus	push	and
yuk	the	stuck	in	muck